HEAVENLY

ENCOUNTERS SERIES: Volume 2

YOUR HIDDEN DESTINY REVEALED

ENCOUNTERING GOD'S HIDDEN STRATEGY FOR YOUR LIFE

D1314081

KEVIN L. ZADAI

WARRIORNOTES

DEDICATION

I dedicate this to the Lord Jesus Christ. When I died during surgery and met with Jesus on the other side, He insisted I return to life on the earth and that I help people with their destinies. Because of Jesus's love and concern for people, He would actually send someone back to let them know that their destiny and purpose is secure in Him. I want you to know Lord, that when You come to take me to be with you someday, I hope that people remember the revelation of Jesus Christ, and not me. I am merely being obedient to the heavenly calling and mission of my Lord, Jesus.

Table of Contents

KEVIN L. ZADAI

ACKNOWLEDGMENTS

In addition to sharing my story with everyone through the book, "Heavenly Visitation: A Guide to the Supernatural" and "Days of Heaven on Earth: A Guide to the Days Ahead", the Lord gave me a commission to produce this book, *Your Hidden Destiny Revealed*. This book addresses some of the revelations concerning the areas that Jesus reviewed and revealed to me, through the Word of God, and by the Spirit of God, during several visitations. I want to thank everyone who has encouraged me, assisted me, and prayed for me during the writing of this work, especially my spiritual parents, Dr. Jesse Duplantis and Dr. Cathy Duplantis. Special thanks to my wonderful wife Kathi, for her love and dedication to the Lord and to me. Thank you, Sid Roth and staff, for your love of the our supernatural Messiah, Jesus . Thank you, Dr. Janet Kline, for the wonderful job editing this book. Thank you, James and Taryn Cabase, for your support of this project. Special thanks, as well, to all my friends who know how to pray and enter into *Your Hidden Destiny Revealed*.

Chapter 1

God's Secret Strategy Concerning Eden

THE PREEMPTIVE STRATEGY OF GOD

Sometimes, we are overly concerned about our circumstances. We worry about how we are going to resolve the issues that have come up because of the enemy's attacks. Then, to make matters even worse, we start to worry on behalf of God and try to second guess how He is going to resolve the dilemma, we find ourselves there because of the strategic attacks of our enemy, Satan.

I have good news for you. Not only does God know about the attacks concerning you, that exist in your present situation, He also knows all of the attacks that will come against you in the future. He has already given you hidden strategies in order to defeat the enemy, as well as hidden strategies that will force him to pay you back, plus extra retribution payments. Make sure you have this clear in your mind: **Nothing catches the Almighty God by surprise.**

THE CREATION PHASE

As we read the creation account in the book of Genesis, we are amazed at the power of the Almighty God demonstrated in this creation phase. God Himself was considering everything that He desired to create. He imagined everything exactly as He wanted it, and He believed completely in His heart that what He said would come to pass would occur. According to the belief God had, He spoke the worlds into existence. The worlds were framed this way. "By faith we understand that the worlds were framed by the word of God, so that the things which are seen were not made of things which are visible (Hebrews 11:3 emphasis added)."

After the six days (phases) of creation were finished, God Almighty paused and considered all that He had done. There were no flaws in that which He created. God Almighty then took time to sanctify and celebrate the end result. He was not tired, but wanted to reflect. "Then God blessed the seventh day and sanctified it, because in it He rested from all His work which God had created and made (Genesis 2:3)."

DISOBEDIENCE

Now the serpent was more cunning than any beast of the field which the Lord God had made. And he said to the woman, "Has God indeed said, 'You shall not eat of every tree of the garden'?" And the woman said to the serpent, "We may eat the fruit of the trees of the garden; but of the fruit of the tree which is in the midst of the garden, God has said, 'You shall not eat it, nor shall you touch it, lest you die.' " Then the serpent said to the woman, "You will not surely die. For God knows that in the day you eat of it your eyes will be opened, and you will be like God, knowing good and evil." So when the woman saw that the tree was good for food, that it was pleasant to the eyes, and a tree desirable to make one wise, she took of its fruit and ate. She also gave to her husband with her, and he ate. Then the eyes of both of them were opened, and they knew that they were naked; and they sewed fig leaves together and made themselves coverings. And they heard the sound of the Lord God walking in the garden in the cool of the day, and Adam and his wife hid themselves from the presence of the Lord God among the trees of the garden. Then the Lord God called to Adam and said to him, "Where are you?" So he said, "I heard Your voice in the garden, and I was afraid because I was naked; and I hid myself." And He said, "Who told you that you were naked? Have you eaten from the tree of which I commanded you that you should not eat (Genesis 3:1-11)?"

The tree was not in the garden for man to be tempted. The tree was placed in the garden so that God Almighty had food to eat from when He visited with man. God wanted to fellowship with men; He came every day to speak with Adam and Eve.

This story is probably very familiar to you, so I will not spend much time on the obvious. There are some things that Jesus revealed to me on which I would like to concentrate. The fact that God knew that man's disobedience was going to happen long before he actually transgressed. Although God knew that man was going to disobey, that fact did not keep God from putting the tree of good and evil in the garden. The tree was not in the garden for man to be tempted. The tree was put there for God Almighty to eat from when He visited with man. God wanted to fellowship with man and came down every day. The only requirement was that man could not eat from the tree of the knowledge of good and evil. You see, the eyes of Adam and Eve where open already. God made man in His image. So you see they were already like God.

God is the only one who can know both good and evil and still choose good. If Man knows good and evil, he will not be able to only choose good.

The serpent attempted to twist the truth so that Adam and Eve felt as if they did not have everything that God had to offer. They felt as though God had left them out of certain things. They were not aware they had everything already. Since we, as humans, were made in the image of God, we are created in God's likeness, but we are not God Himself. God is the only One who could know both good and evil and still choose good. If Man knows good and evil, he is incapable of only choosing good. That knowledge of evil corrupts us. We feel tempted to explore evil. We should never have known evil, but now we do because we are fallen beings.

Since we, as humans were made in the image of God, we are created in God's likeness, but we are not God Himself.

So the entrance of sin came through disobedience of what God has required. The reason for the disobedience was because mankind was deceived into thinking that they did not have everything that they could posses. As a result of this deception, they believed they were somehow left out. This was not the case at all. So remember, you cannot know both good and evil and always choose good, unless you are God Himself. That is why mankind became corrupted.

MAN'S SOLUTION

Man's solution to the problem was to shift the blame of disobedience from himself to someone else. That is often still how we deal with our problems. We would rather blame others than be held accountable for our failures. So after the blame was shifted several times, man was even ignorant to extent that he began to blame God.

After realizing that they were naked, Adam and Eve thought that they had to help God in the dilemma they created. So they grabbed the nearest thing to cover themselves, the leaves of the fig tree. They used the leaves from the fig tree to hide the problem. They wanted to solve God's problem for Him, as well as solve their own problems for themselves. They attempted to solve their own problems by shifting the blame from themselves.

The God Almighty was revealing His hidden strategy that was already planned for mankind. God had all ready determined that His Son would die for mankind as an expression of His love.

When God came down to walk with them in the garden, but could not find them. He called for them, and when He found them, He asked them why they were hiding. He already knew what had happened, but He still wanted to talk to them face-to-face. You see, God already had a solution, but it was not a solution that man could provide. The fig leaves were not the solution that was chosen by God. The Lord provided animal skins for them. The skins came from animals that were in the garden. Their lives were sacrificed so that Adam and Eve could be covered the way that God chose for them to be covered; They were covered by the shedding of blood. God Almighty was revealing His hidden strategy that He had already planned for mankind. God had all ready determined, long ago, that His Son would die for mankind as an expression of His love. The fact that Jesus died on a cross was not plan "B" because plan "A" had failed. God's plan clearly demonstrates His hidden strategy that Jesus was slain from the foundation of the world. God was getting man ready for the redemption process when He killed those animals and gave them the skins to wear. As we know, He later revealed the blood sacrifice to Moses and instituted it for the children of Israel. God, once again, was not caught off guard.

Jesus told me the reason that He cursed the fig tree was to reveal His plan for mankind. He came back, not only to destroy the effects of sin on mankind by redemption, but also because He hates the teachings of any religion that attributes man's way of dealing with our spiritual condition. Men's way is to restrict the flesh, which has absolutely no effect upon the root of the problem, which originates not in man's flesh, but in his spirit. This was what the religion of the day taught. The Pharisees also taught that sin can be overcome by only dealing with the flesh; they overlooked the need for man's spirit to be redeemed. The Apostle Paul said, "...having a form of godliness but denying its power. And from such people turn away! For of this sort are those who creep into households and make captives of gullible women loaded down with sins, led away by various lusts, always learning and never able to come to the knowledge of the truth (2 Timothy 3:5-8 emphasis added)."

GOD'S SOLUTION

Jesus knew that He was the Solution, so He confronted any form of religion that made man come under bondage and oppression, and therefore, had no real spiritual solution. I have met Jesus on several occasions. I am testifying in my writings concerning His character and personality constantly. He hates religion because it takes the place of a personal relationship with the Father. He came to seek and save those who are lost (see Luke 19:10).

**The fig tree represented man's way
of covering sin. When He saw the fig tree did not have
any fruit, it reminded Him of the teachings of the
Pharisees and all religion.**

The Apostle Matthew quotes Jesus saying, "The scribes and the Pharisees sit in Moses' seat. Therefore whatever they tell you to observe, that observe and do, but do not do according to their works; for they say, and do not do. For they bind heavy burdens, hard to bear, and lay them on men's shoulders; but they themselves will not move them with one of their fingers. Woe to you, scribes and Pharisees, hypocrites! For you travel land and sea to win one proselyte, and when he is won, you make him twice as much a son of hell as yourselves. Woe to you, scribes and Pharisees, hypocrites! For you pay tithe of mint and anise and cummin, and have neglected the weightier matters of the law: justice and mercy and faith. These you ought to have done, without leaving the others undone. Blind guides, who strain out a gnat and swallow a camel! Woe to you, scribes and Pharisees, hypocrites! For you cleanse the outside of the cup and dish, but inside they are full of extortion and self-indulgence. Blind Pharisee, first cleanse the inside of the cup and dish, that the outside of them may be clean also. Woe to you, scribes and Pharisees, hypocrites! For you are like whitewashed tombs which indeed appear beautiful outwardly, but inside are full of dead men's bones and all uncleanness. Even so you also outwardly appear righteous to men, but inside you are full of hypocrisy and lawlessness (Matthew 23:2-4,15, 23-28)."

The fig tree represented man's way of covering sin. When Jesus saw the fig tree did not have any fruit, it reminded Him of the teachings of the Pharisees, as well as the teachings of all religions. It reminded Him of what happened in the garden of Eden when Adam and Eve disobeyed His command and ate of the tree of the knowledge of good and evil, and then grabbed the leaves of the tree to cover themselves. He knew that they were dealing with the problem that they had created, in their own way. That is exactly the same reason that He cursed the fig tree at the roots. He came back to destroy all the works of the devil and to bring the offspring of Adam and Eve back to God through His own sacrifice. God has revealed His hidden strategy. It was revealed to Adam and Eve in the garden of Eden. God let the serpent (satan) know that he was doomed. God reveals that someday the seed of the woman, Mary, will have a baby. That baby, Jesus, will get His heel bruised. However, then He will bruise the head of the serpent.

"And I will put enmity
between you and the woman,
and between your seed and her Seed; He shall
bruise your head, and you shall bruise His
heel (Genesis 3:15)."

So, even before the creation of the world, it was revealed that God would work this plan of salvation concerning His Son. Sin was not putting God in a corner. God had planned to reveal His love for us through the death of His Son.

Chapter 2

God's Secret Strategy Concerning Adam

The events that happened in the Garden of Eden eventually led to Adam and Eve being forcefully escorted out of the beautiful Paradise of provision and protection. They were in a self-inflicted dilemma and needed an Advocate. We know that Jesus was already slain from the foundation of the world. According to Scripture, "All who dwell on the earth will worship him, whose names have not been written in the Book of Life of the Lamb slain from the foundation of the world (Revelation 13:8 emphasis added)." There is a Book of Life, and you are written in it because you are one of the redeemed.

God Almighty secretly chose all of Adam's descendants and their names before the foundations of the world. He told us what He was going to do for mankind for the next six thousand years.

What would you think if I told you that God has hidden His secret strategies in the lineage of Adam? God Almighty secretly chose all of Adam's descendants and their names before Adam was even created. He told us what He was going to do for mankind for the next six thousand years. God always has a secret strategy for our lives that will completely defeat the enemy! God is still working in the Earth to provide every victory in your life, in every circumstance no matter what battle may arise. The mighty Spirit of the living God has anointed you for this hour of destiny. You were created in the image of God, and Jesus has restored you to that image. Our flesh may wear out, but we can be healed by the new covenant of the blood of Jesus. You will live forever now, regardless of your flesh, because of Jesus. Remember this truth: You are made in His image!

" In the day that God created man, he made him in the likeness of God (Genesis 5;1)."

We need to be reminded that Adam lived for a long time, even after his sinful condition started working against him. Adam was able to live such a long life because he was created in the image of God, Even sin could not defeat Adam's physical body for a very long time. In our time, we feel blessed to live over one hundred years. This is far from the nine hundred thirty years Adam lived. "This is the book of the genealogy of Adam. In the day that God created man, he made him in the likeness of God. He created them male and female, And blessed them and called them Mankind in the day that they were created. And Adam lived 130 years, And begot a son in his own likeness, after his image, and named him Seth. After he begot Seth, the days of Adam where eight hundred years; and he had sons and daughters. So all the days that Adam lived were 930 years; and he died (Genesis 5:1-5 emphasis added)."

The Names and Their Meanings in the Genealogy of Genesis, Chapter Five.

Name:	Meaning:
Adam	Man
Seth	Appointed
Enosh	Mortal
Kenan	Sorrow
Mahalalel	The Blessed God
Jared	Shall come down
Enoch	Teaching
Methuselah	His death shall bring
Lamech	The Despairing
Noah	Rest, comfort

Here is what happens to the genealogy, if you take all the meanings of the names and make a sentence out of them; keeping them in order.

Man appointed mortal sorrow; the Blessed God shall come down, teaching, His death shall bring the despairing rest and comfort.

The genealogy becomes a revelation of God's plan for man. The Almighty God knows the end from the beginning! I have several questions for you. How much more does God know about you, that is hidden in a secret stategy against the enemy? What will be revealed to show that God has rigged your life in your favor? If He can do what was just shown to you, what else can He do that is not shown? He truly knows the end from the beginning, and He wants to show you favor!

**Remember the former things of old,
For I am God, and there is no other; I am God,
and there is none like Me, declaring the end from the
beginning, and from ancient times things that are
not yet done, saying, 'My counsel shall stand,
And I will do all My pleasure,' (Isaiah 46:9-10
emphasis added).**

Chapter 3

God's Secret Strategy Concerning Enoch

**Faith lifted Enoch from this life
and he was taken up into heaven! He never had to
experience death; he just disappeared from this world
because God promoted him. For before he was
translated to the heavenly realm his life had
become a pleasure to God (He had a
reputation of pleasing God
Hebrews 11:5 TPT emphasis
added)**

Enoch was another secret weapon of God Almighty. God
used Enoch to prepare the way for the flood that occurred
during the time of Noah. Enoch was a preacher of
righteousness that prophesied the second coming of the
Lord. Enoch, the seventh direct descendant from Adam,
prophesied of their doom when he said, " Look! Here comes

the Lord Yahweh with his countless myriads of holy ones. He comes to execute judgment against them all and to convict each one of them for their ungodly deeds and for all their terrible words that ungodly sinners have spoken against him (Jude 1:14,15 TPT emphasis added)."

Enoch was a powerful prophet that went around warning all those who had interbred with the Nephilim, who were present in those days. The world was so corrupt that God repented that He had created man and beast. There was so much sexual sin that hybrid beings were being created. These beings were sometimes more creature-like than human.

Then the people began to multiply on the earth, and daughters were born to them. The sons of God saw the beautiful women and took any they wanted as their wives. Then the Lord said, "My Spirit will not put up with humans for such a long time, for they are only mortal flesh. In the future, their normal lifespan will be no more than 120 years. "In those days, and for some time after, giant Nephilites lived on the earth, for whenever the sons of God had intercourse with women, they gave birth to children who became the heroes and famous warriors of ancient times. The Lord observed the extent of human wickedness on the earth, and he saw that everything they thought or imagined was consistently and totally evil. **So the Lord was sorry he had ever made them and put them on the earth. It broke his heart.** And the Lord said, "I will wipe this human race I have created from the face of the earth. Yes, and I will destroy every living thing—all the people, the large animals, the small animals that scurry along the ground, and even the birds of the sky. I am sorry I ever made them." But Noah found favor with the Lord (Genesis 6:1-8 NLT emphasis added).

Can you imagine having to prophesy to these corrupt hybrids? God used Enoch and his intimate walk with Him to warn and eventually cause judgment to come on the earth and its inhabitants. Judgment came upon all except Noah and his family; there were eight people in his family.

The Almighty God already knew that He would have to destroy every living thing on the earth. But He was not caught off guard. God caused Enoch to walk in such power. I saw Enoch once, and He was walking in the power of the resurrection with God just as Jesus wants us to walk with Him. Even in a wicked and perverse generation that requires a sign, we can walk with God in power and proclaim the message of reconciliation to this world before the end comes. If you will just receive the impartation that Jesus gave me and the angel that escorted me in this encounter, the impartation that He has released to me to give out, you could be set free right now!

ENCOUNTERING ENOCH

On October 16th, a couple of years ago, on my wife Kathi's birthday, we were on an airplane traveling to Seattle. I was wearing my headsets and I was on the aisle seat in the airplane. Someone came and stood beside me in the aisle. I opened my eyes, and the power of God hit me. Even though I did not see anybody there initially, all of a sudden, I could see that there was an angel standing there beside me in the aisle. He grabbed me and took me, and we left the airplane. We went so fast. He had me by the arm, and away we went. We landed in a forest, in an area where a field opened up. I did not know where we were. I saw a man who was fairly short walking on the path in front of us. He had some sort of garment on. It appeared to be the skin of an animal.

The angel said, "I have been given permission to show you the powers of the Coming Age." He said, "Watch!" He pointed to the man as the man took one more step. The resurrection power just burst around the man on the path, as he stepped through, to the realm of the Heavenly. His name was Enoch. The power that came out from him as he went through that last step into the heavenly realm was so strong, that it came back and hit me and the angel. That Power burst through us forcefully. It was so bright and so powerful.

Then he said, "Come." Then the angel took me and we went to another place very quickly. I saw another man standing there. A chariot came up and he got on it. Then, the same thing happened again. There was a burst of resurrection power; it was the same power that raised Jesus from the dead, and it burst around him. He disappeared. The blast came back, and it hit us once again. It was so strong! Then the angel turned to me and handed me a scroll which I do not have, because it is in the Bible. He said, "You need to read II Corinthians, chapter 5, especially verse 17. You have been called to a ministry of reconciliation. You have been shown the powers of the Coming Age so that you can participate in it right now." He said, "People just need to be told that they have been bought, and that all of humanity has been bought and purchased. They just need to be told that the price for man has already been paid for. You tell them that God has purchased them through Jesus Christ, and that this is the powers of the coming age." He then took me back to forty thousand feet, and put me in my seat on the right airplane and left.

THE ANGEL'S WORD

It is the ministry of reconciliation! The resurrection is so strong that when you testify, it raises people from the dead, and they come back to life right before your eyes as you announce this Good News to them. It was explained to me why the testimony of Jesus is the spirit of prophecy:

> And I fell at his feet to worship him. But he said
> to me, "See that you do not do that! I am your

fellow servant, and of your brethren who have the testimony of Jesus. Worship God! For the testimony of Jesus is the spirit of prophecy." Revelation 19:10 NKJV

When you start to talk about Jesus, it gets into prophecy because the Spirit wants to testify and take over. When you start talking about Jesus, the Holy Spirit automatically manifests every time.

I realized that the resurrection power that is dwelling in me wants to raise people from the dead. I can spiritually raise people from the dead just by testifying of Jesus; it initiates that resurrection power. It is called the ministry of reconciliation. The angel had given me a scroll, but I did not have it when I came back. It was the whole fifth chapter of II Corinthians. He said I needed to learn this. He said, "You need to learn the whole chapter, especially in the area of verses 15 and 17."

For the love of Christ compels us, because we judge thus: that if One died for all, then all died; and He died for all, that those who live should live no longer for themselves, but for Him who died for them and rose again. Therefore, from now on, we regard no one according to the flesh. Even though we have known Christ according to the flesh, yet now we know Him thus no longer. Therefore, if anyone is in Christ, he is a new creation; old things have passed away; behold, all things have become new. Now all things are of God, who has reconciled us to Himself through Jesus Christ, and has given us the ministry of reconciliation, that is, that God was in Christ reconciling the world to Himself, not imputing their trespasses to them, and has committed to us the word of reconciliation. Now then, we are ambassadors for Christ, as though God were pleading through us:

we implore you on Christ's behalf, be reconciled to God. For He made Him who knew no sin to be sin for us, that we might become the righteousness of God in Him. (2 Cor. 5:14-21 emphasis added).

ENOCH'S PROFILE

Here are some facts about Enoch:

1. He lived three hundred sixty-five years.

2. He started walking with God at age sixty-five.

3. He walked with God three hundred years.

4. He was a prophet that prophesied (See Jude 14).

5. He pleased God and was taken away with Him. (See Heb.11:5)

6. Enoch was seventh generation from Adam (See Jude 14).

"As were the days of Noah, so will be the coming of the Son of Man" (Matt 24:37 AMP).

The parallel to this is that Enoch was caught away. He walked with God, and he was not. That catching away is representative of what will happen with the church. So the church, in the age where we are presently living, is a dispensation where God has focused on His body through the Church. That is the point where the church is found right now. The change is coming, and soon that dispensation will end. This age is to follow the same pattern as that of the life and ministry of Enoch. Our walk involves the same pattern as the walk of Enoch possessed.

Chapter 4

God's Secret Strategy Concerning Noah

From the beginning it was preplanned that Noah would succeed. This follows the same pattern that we have already discussed thus far. As we have seen in the genealogy of Genesis chapter five, the Gospel message was within, long before anyone could be aware of that secret. Right now, at this minute, God knows your destiny and what hidden strategy is hidden in your name and genealogy. We must concentrate on the long-term goals that God has for your life, and not focus upon the difficulties or struggles that we now happen to be encountering at the present time.

I have something else to share concerning Noah. What I have to reveal shows that God had a hidden strategy against the enemy concerning the human race. I am sure this will help you. The strategy is hidden in the following verses.

One of the first things that I want to point out to you is what Jesus revealed to me about the placement of the water and how it was positioned by God during creation. Water was placed in the earth in such a way that God could make it available as a secret weapon against Lucifer later. "Then God said, 'Let there be a space between the waters, to separate the waters of the heavens from the waters of the earth.' And that is what happened. God made this space to separate the waters of the earth from the waters of the heavens. And evening passed and morning came, marking the second day (Genesis 1:6-8 NLT)."

The Lord told me that He had hidden the water under the ground in caverns. It did not rain until the depths of the earth released their storage of water at the Lord's command. This command was given as soon Noah was safely in the ark.

The earth was watered from underneath. Rain did not fall upon the plants of the earth. The whole Garden of Eden was watered by these springs. "When the Lord God made the earth and the heavens, neither wild plants nor grains were growing on the earth. The Lord God had not yet sent rain to water the earth, and there were no people to cultivate the soil. Instead, springs came up from the ground and watered all the land. Then the Lord God formed the man from the dust of the ground (Genesis 2:4-6 emphasis added)."

I was amazed when I was told how corrupt the world had become during the time before the flood. Men and animals had been genetically altered through interbreeding. The corruption was so worldwide that God had a broken heart and even repented that He had created man. The violence became so intolerable that God announced that He had suffered this corruption long enough. "Now God saw that the earth had become corrupt and was filled with violence. God observed all this corruption in the world, for everyone on earth was corrupt. So God said to Noah, 'I have decided to destroy all living creatures, for they have filled the earth with violence. Yes, I will wipe them all out along with the earth (Gen 6:11-13 emphasis)!' "

One of the secret weapons that God had was actually in Noah. Just like the Christians of today, Noah had a gift of evangelism. He warned the people of the coming judgment before it happened. The people had interbred with beings that were fallen from their proper place in God. Animals had become corrupted as well. The Apostle Peter said, "...and did not spare the ancient world, but saved Noah, one of eight people, a preacher of righteousness, bringing in the flood on the world of the ungodly (2 Peter 2:5)." Noah and his family had kept themselves from the interbreeding. He was a man that feared God and was kept pure in a corrupt world. The Bible testifies that He was a preacher of righteousness.

Noah was part of God's secret weaponry. You, also, are part of God's hidden strategy again in this age. Jesus referred to the world's condition being the same as the days of Noah when He returns for His Bride (see Matthew 24:37). That is why I was sent back from the dead; **I was sent back to activate people for the final days of this dispensation.** God is about to pour out His Spirit on all flesh and we are going to see His Glory.

Moses, who wrote the book of Genesis, gave this testimony, years later, "Noah was a just man, perfect in his generations. Noah walked with God (Genesis 6:9)."

The word used there for generations in this verse, has to do with a word that means **genetics** today. He, and his family, were not part of the hybrid race of people on the earth.

After Noah had preached to the hybrid race of people and finished building the ark, God told him to go inside the ark and wait. God's secret strategy for the enemy, Lucifer, was about to be revealed. The water that He had placed and what was hidden underground, for this very moment, was released. "When Noah was six hundred years old, on the seventeenth day of the second month, all the underground waters erupted from the earth, and the rain fell in mighty torrents from the sky. The rain continued to fall for forty days and forty nights (Genesis 7:11-12 NLT)."

Lucifer thought that he had corrupted the human race, and he therefore assumed that he had stopped the prophecy that was spoken to him in the Garden of Eden, which was, "And I will put enmity between you and the woman, **and between your seed and her Seed**; He shall bruise your head, and you shall bruise His heel (Genesis 3:15)." You see, Lucifer thought that the Messiah would be corrupted because of the interbreeding. Jesus had to be a " Spotless Lamb." If He had any hybrid blood in His genealogy, Jesus would not be completely human and that fact would disqualify Him from being a perfect sacrifice for mankind.

God had beaten Lucifer on two fronts. One place of victory was that God was able to preserve the genetics of Noah and his family. Secondly, God was able to preserve the water under the surface of the earth until the time came to destroy every living thing. God has never been put in "checkmate". He told me this, "I have never been put in checkmate. I always reserve the last move for Myself." In this case, He was well able to circumvent the enemy in a major way and thereby obtain complete victory!

Chapter 5

God's Secret Strategy Concerning Moses

There is an abundance of information about Moses in the Bible. When I was with Jesus, He referred to Moses in examples as He was teaching me. The example of Moses will reveal God's secret strategies concerning His plan for mankind.

As you know from the history of the Children of Israel, they became enslaved after Joseph died. He had been one of the main leaders of Egypt. He had been sent ahead as a deliver for God's people. Many of you have been sent ahead, just as Joseph, to be a catalyst for what God is doing for the generation to whom you are called . Moses was one of those people. He was God's secret weapon for

25

the great deliverance from slavery in which he and his people had found themselves. In fear that Moses would be killed because of Pharaoh's decree to kill all babies of a certain age, his mother sent him afloat on the Nile river as a newborn. It was a divine setup because Moses was found by one of Pharaoh's court attendants. Moses grew up there with Pharaoh's daughter as his guardian, learning the ways of Pharaoh and Egypt for God's future plan. It was a divine plan for him to be groomed in Pharaoh's court.

This is similar to your life: you sometimes wonder why you are involved with the job you are presently enduring or the school that you attend. Do not forget about the hidden agenda of Heaven! The book of Hebrews testifies of the faith of Moses and God's hidden plan:

> By faith Moses, when he was born, was hidden three months by his parents, because they saw he was a beautiful child; and they were not afraid of the king's command. By faith Moses, when he became of age, refused to be called the son of Pharaoh's daughter, choosing rather to suffer affliction with the people of God than to enjoy the passing pleasures of sin, esteeming the reproach of Christ greater riches than the treasures in Egypt; for he looked to the reward. By faith he forsook Egypt, not fearing the wrath of the king; for he endured as seeing Him who is invisible. By faith he kept the Passover and the sprinkling of blood, lest he who destroyed the firstborn should touch them. By faith they passed through the Red Sea as by dry land, whereas the Egyptians, attempting to do so, were drowned (Hebrews 11:23-29).

HARD CHOICES

The Holy Spirit has been called alongside us to help us to make decisions in every area of our lives. Trusting God in all of our hard places of struggling difficulty creates permanent faith and character. Moses had to choose between the riches and passing pleasures of being a son of Pharaoh's daughter, and serving the God of the Jewish people. The choices we encounter sometimes involve counting the cost. Moses' destiny and purpose cost him dearly.

We must remember this fact: you are "seeing Him who is invisible." I have seen Jesus and the realm of the Spirit. Because of my experiences with Jesus and the realm of the Spirit, I must encourage you in all things pertaining to our Lord Jesus Christ and the Heavenly Realm. There is nothing worth more than to behold Him and to please Him then the conscious choice of and continuous living in faith on the earth. There is a greater reward for those who have not seen Him but still believe in Him (see John 20:29).

GOD'S SECRET AGENT

Moses chose to live his life for God. He was chosen before the events took place that could have destroyed his people to deliver Israel at an opportune time. When God decided long before the Israelites were even in Egypt, to deliver them through the leadership of Moses, He wrote about Moses and his days, in the books on the shelves of Heaven's library (see Psalms 139:16). Moses felt the call to deliver his people from their oppression so intensely that he was at the point of frustration. Finally he acted on that frustration, and he killed an Egyptian in his anger.

Be submissive to the Holy Spirit's impartation as you read this book. Allow the examples used in this book to help you as you wait on God's timing for your destiny to begin to be implemented in your life.

Moses had to flee into the desert to keep from being killed. God knew that Moses would have to flee ahead of time. God used this opportunity to plan Moses' training for the "Exodus" out of Egypt. Jesus personally discussed this training of Moses with me. God explained that the training of Moses was a prerequisite for how effective Moses would be when the time came for Moses to fulfill his role in the destiny of the nation of Israel.

Jesus revealed to me, with the assistance of the Holy Spirit, that both the forty years in the courts of Pharaoh and the forty years in the Midian desert, were a divine plan that prepared Moses to be used in one of the most profound demonstrations of God Almighty on record. No other people witnessed the acts of God as the Children of Israel did. No single man saw the Glory of God, and had the ways of God revealed, in the Old Testament, as Moses. "He made known His ways to Moses, His acts to the children of Israel (Psalms 103:7)."

The Spirit is saying to you, "Trust me as I prepare you for your destiny. No preparation seems easy at the time, but remember that I am more focused on your character in this season than your comfort. The comfort will always follow hard times. I, the Lord, can only take you as far as your character will allow!"

In the first forty years, the management skills and education that Moses received in Egypt were the best in the world at that time. The survival skills and ability to navigate effectively in the Midian desert were also needed later as he led millions of people through, what was to Him, familiar territory.

Many times, the Lord has told me to do something for Him that was not on my own agenda. He would always say to me, "You do not understand this now, but later on you will see." I can testify that this has been the truth every time.

I remember attending the university to achieve my Bachelor degree. I had been so diligent that I had finished my degree in three, instead of the usual four years years. I felt the urgency to go on to my next set of training, which was another two-year program. This program was beyond what I had just accomplished. As I was getting fitted for my gown and for the ceremony, The Lord asked me, "What are you doing". I said, "I'm graduating from the college that You told me to attend." He reminded me that a year prior He had asked me to get two other degrees of study as well. I had not obeyed Him because I was not interested in the two subjects that He gave me. He said to me, "You don't understand this now, but later you will. You are going to need to know the information given to you for these degrees." I was very puzzled because one of the degrees was music and the other degree was journalism. He asked me to get minors in these disciplines. I was not interested in music or in journalism, so I refused to take all the classes that the Lord had told me to take because I did not do very well in some of them. I walked out of the fitting room and reestablished my course of studies for one more year. I did not graduate and then as I had planned, but stayed to complete those areas of study as God had told me to do initially. After that year, I graduated with my class, and I had taken those areas of study. Several years ago when I came back from my heavenly experience in the operating room, I could therefore play musical instruments without having lessons. He asked me to start writing books about my experiences and to help people by teaching and writing what he had shown me in books. It was just as the the Lord said. I did not know at the time how important this was but now I realize how important it was to follow his instructions concerning those additional areas of study.

That is why I share this with you now. I know that there are many of you who do not see the big picture as Moses and I failed at first to see it. You need to seek the Lord and hear His voice. Be certain to do as the Lord requests, even if it doesn't make sense at the time. Most of what you have gone through this far in life is just preparation for what He has for you to accomplish for Him. Be obedient right now in your preparation. God's not wasting your life. He is hiding you until the proper time so that you can fulfill the destiny that He has prepared for you.

WHAT IS IN YOUR HAND

There are times, because of our progress in the maturity process and in yielding to God's training in our life, that we may hear God say, "You do something about it"! It may shock you quite a bit when God speaks to you in such a bold and direct manner. I have learned, and I want to teach you, that when God puts such a demand upon your life, it is generally a very good sign. It shows that God has already rigged it in your favor, and that He trusts you. Moses had to learn the ways of God step-by-step. When God appeared to Moses, He gave Him some instructions:

> Then Moses answered and said, But suppose they will not believe me or listen to my voice; suppose they say, 'The Lord has not appeared to you.' So the Lord said to him, 'What is that in your hand?' He said, 'A rod.' And He said, "Cast it on the ground." So he cast it on the ground, and it became a serpent; and Moses fled from it. Then the Lord said to Moses, 'Reach out your hand and take it by the tail' (and he reached out his hand and caught it, and it became a rod in his hand), 'that they may believe that the Lord God of their fathers, the God of Abraham, the God of Isaac, and the God of Jacob, has appeared to you (Exodus 4:1-5).'

This instruction was very convincing to Moses and so he used it as a sign to Pharaoh. This was to prove to Pharaoh that the Lord was with Moses. However, when the sign was performed, the magicians did the same thing. That is when Moses' rod, that had turned into a serpent, ate up the magicians' rods. It was not until the Israelites arrived at the

Red Sea that Moses once again was asked by God, "What is in your hand?"

> But Moses told the people, "Don't be afraid. Just stand still and watch the Lord rescue you today. The Egyptians you see today will never be seen again. The Lord himself will fight for you. Just stay calm." Then the Lord said to Moses, "Why are you crying out to me? Tell the people to get moving! Pick up your staff and raise your hand over the sea. Divide the water so the Israelites can walk through the middle of the sea on dry ground.   And I will harden the hearts of the Egyptians, and they will charge in after the Israelites. My great glory will be displayed through Pharaoh and his troops, his chariots, and his charioteers. When my glory is displayed through them, all Egypt will see my glory and know that I am the Lord (Exodus 14:13-18 NLT)!"

I know that the revelation of the Holy Spirit is flowing now to you as you are beginning to see that Moses was being developed in his faith concerning what was in His hand. He knew that the staff would split the Red Sea. Notice that He did not start there at the Red Sea. Moses began learning God's ways while he was in the desert at the burning bush. He received his instructions from the Lord concerning the staff. That instruction eventually developed into a glorious deliverance in front of an estimated two million people.

CHOSEN

When you are chosen by the Lord for a task, just like Moses, was chosen for a specific task, you may have to learn many lessons. The development of your faith will cause you to eventually operate at full capacity in that victory for which God has chosen you. Along the way, you may feel stretched to the point of discomfort. However, remember that your faith is being developed. "In this you greatly rejoice, though now for a little while, if need be, you have been grieved by various trials, that the genuineness of your faith, being much more precious than gold that perishes, though it is tested by fire, may be found to praise, honor, and glory at the revelation of Jesus Christ, whom having not seen you love (1 Peter 1:6-8)."

FACE TO FACE

As we see later on in the ministry of Moses, God began to bring him up on Mt. Siniai. This involved all kinds of supernatural events that everyone of us would like to have experienced. However, we must also be willing to be stretched in the hard times. Moses experienced at least two, forty-day long fasts on a mountain, and Moses stood face to face with God. These experiences produced such a closeness with the Creator God that Moses' face started to glow in the image of his God!

> Now it was so, when Moses came down from Mount Sinai (and the two tablets of the Testimony were in Moses' hand when he came down from the mountain), that Moses did not know that the skin of his face shone while he talked with Him. So when Aaron and all the children of Israel saw Moses, behold, the skin of his face shone, and they were afraid to come near him. Then Moses called to them, and Aaron and all the rulers of the congregation returned to him; and Moses talked with them. Afterward all the children of Israel came near, and he gave them as commandments all that the Lord had spoken with him on Mount Sinai. And when Moses had finished speaking with them, he put a veil on his face. But whenever Moses went in before the Lord to speak with Him, he would take the veil off until he came

out; and he would come out and speak to the children of Israel whatever he had been commanded. And whenever the children of Israel saw the face of Moses, that the skin of Moses' face shone, then Moses would put the veil on his face again, until he went in to speak with Him (Exodus 34:29-35 emphasis added).

Moses was very instrumental in the implementation of God's plan for His people. The Lord had even allowed people to come up and meet with Him. Moses was the only one that responded to the invitation. This was wonderful. Moses was able to get so close with Him. Moses even convinced God to deal mercifully with His people. In this way, God's reputation would not be tarnished among the Egyptians (see Exodus 32:11,12). Moses had become so close to God in the relationship, that God listened to him when He spoke.

"So the Lord spoke to Moses face to face, as a man speaks to his friend (Exodus 33:11)."

GLORY

One of the most awesome events that God did for Moses was to reveal the Glory. Moses had experienced His presence. God had told him that His presence would go with Him. Moses was not satisfied with just knowing that God's presence would abide with him. He somehow knew that there was more to God, as a Person, than what was known. Moses asked God to show him His Glory. According to God, this was not an easy thing because Moses would lose his life over it apparently!

And He said, "My Presence will go with you, and I will give you rest." Then he said to Him, "If Your Presence does not go with us, do not bring us up from here. For how then will it be known that Your

33

people and I have found grace in Your sight, except You go with us? So we shall be separate, Your people and I, from all the people who are upon the face of the earth." So the Lord said to Moses, "I will also do this thing that you have spoken; for you have found grace in My sight, and I know you by name." And he said, "Please, show me Your glory." Then He said, "I will make all My goodness pass before you, and I will proclaim the name of the Lord before you. I will be gracious to whom I will be gracious, and I will have compassion on whom I will have compassion." But He said, "You cannot see My face; for no man shall see Me, and live." And the Lord said, "Here is a place by Me, and you shall stand on the rock. So it shall be, while My glory passes by, that I will put you in the cleft of the rock, and will cover you with My hand while I pass by. Then I will take away My hand, and you shall see My back; but My face shall not be seen (Exodus 33:14-23)."

"I am praying not only for these disciples but also for all who will ever believe in me through their message. I pray that they will all be one, just as you and I are one—as you are in me, Father, and I am in you. And may they be in us so that the world will believe you sent me. "I have given them the glory you gave me, so they may be one as we are one. I am in them and you are in me. May they experience such perfect unity that the world will know that you sent me and that you love them as much as you love me. Father, I want these whom you have given me to be with me where I am. Then they can see all the glory you gave me because you loved me even before the world began (John 17:20-24 NLT emphasis added)!

"I have given them the glory You gave me, so they may be one as We are one."

34

Jesus Christ

Chapter 6

God's Secret Strategy Concerning Elijah

$\mathcal{G}$od has always used the prophet to foretell the future based on the revelation of God's intentions for the people. Prophets seem to flow with God as a living example of what God is saying and doing. Prophets see and hear what is going on in the Spirit Realm. Jesus referred to His ministry as One that sees what His Father is doing, and then acts. He also said that He is One that hears what His Father is saying, then speaks. Elijah was such a prophet. He would see into the Spirit Realm and act or speak accordingly. Elijah was very bold about the Word of the Lord. He would do the most profound things that shocked most people. Elijah walked with God in a profound way. He was not hesitant to confront anything ungodly that was against the revealed will of God.

As mentioned in a previous chapter, I was able to see Elijah taken up in the chariot of God. Elijah did not see death. The power that was surrounding him as he was translated was beyond description. I was shown this because I was asking the Lord Jesus about the phrase, "...tasted of the powers of the Coming Age" (See Hebrews 6:5).

THE WORD OF THE LORD

One of God's secret strategies that He executes against the enemy, is the Word of the Lord. God rose up Elijah at a time when correction needed to come against any evil in the Land. The other function of the Word of the Lord is for the implementation of God in the lives of the godly. At times, we all need to have confirmation from Heaven, through a person, concerning what is God's perfect will for our lives. God used Elijah to minister to people. He pronounced judgment and blessings while serving God as a prophet. We all know how God used him to stop and start the rain during a period of three-and-one-half years. Elijah would give words of judgment to the wicked kings and their kingdoms. There were even showdowns between Elijah, the prophet of God and the false prophets, who served Baal. God uses this special calling, the office of a prophet, to absolutely enforce the enemies' defeat. I love how God uses people as secret weapons of His destiny. Our purposes are much greater than we can conceive, therefore, We need the Spirit of God to reveal that purpose to us (see 1 Corinthians 2:9, 10).

I like the story of the widow of Zarephath. It not only shows the office and calling of a prophet in action. It also displays the Love of God to a person in need. God uses Elijah in ways such as this throughout his entire ministry. Love and compassion are very powerful secret weapons used by the prophet. The widow received divine ministry because of a faithful prophet named Elijah.

> Then the word of the Lord came to him, saying, "Arise, go to Zarephath, which belongs to Sidon, and dwell there. See, I have commanded a widow there to provide for you." So he arose and went to Zarephath. And when he came to the gate of the city, indeed a widow was there gathering sticks. And he called to her and said, "Please bring me a little water in a cup, that I may drink." And as she was going to get it, he called to her and said, "Please bring me a morsel of bread in your hand." So she said, "As the Lord your God lives, I do not have bread, only a handful of flour in a bin, and a little oil in a jar; and see, I am gathering a couple of sticks that I may go in and prepare it for myself and my son, that we may eat it, and die." And Elijah said to her, "Do not fear; go and do as you have said, but make me a small cake from it first, and bring it to me; and afterward make some for yourself and your son. For thus says the Lord God of Israel: 'The bin of flour shall not be used up, nor shall the jar of oil run dry, until the day the Lord sends rain on the earth.'" So she went away and did according to the word of Elijah; and she and he and her household ate for many days. The bin of flour was not used up, nor did the jar of oil run dry, according to the word of the Lord which He spoke by Elijah (1 Kings 17:8-16).

The Lord wants to use all of us to minister to people in a supernatural way. You might be God's secret weapon to break the power of the devil off someone by just allowing

God to speak to you in prayer. After God uses you in such a manner, you will often see the provision of God flow into peoples' lives supernaturally. Not only will others benefit from that type of situation, but it is probable you, also, will receive provision. When God uses you to tell people, "Do not fear," watch as God confirms His Word with signs following (Hebrews 2:4). God wants to bless His people. That will come when men and women speak the Word of God with great boldness under the leading of the Holy Spirit.

A MAN OF PRAYER

We must note that Elijah was a man of prayer. He knew how to accomplish his mission when he heard from God. I learned from Elijah that we must have an intensity and a fervency while in prayer. The Apostle James spoke well of Elijah when he said this, "The effective, fervent prayer of a righteous man avails much. Elijah was a man with a nature like ours, and he prayed earnestly that it would not rain; and it did not rain on the land for three years and six months. And he prayed again, and the heaven gave rain, and the earth produced its fruit (James 5:16-18 emphasis added)."

THE PROPHETIC HANDOFF

There is a great amount of interest revolving around the office of the prophet. Many want to walk in that office desperately. The Apostle Paul explained that, "**He (God) Himself gave some to be** apostles, **some prophets**, some evangelists, and some pastors and teachers, for the equipping of the saints for the work of ministry, for the edifying of the body of Christ, till we all come to the unity of the faith and of the knowledge of the Son of God, to a perfect man, to the measure of the stature of the fullness of Christ (Ephesians 4:11-14)".

So we just learned from the Apostle Paul's writings that

you cannot appoint yourself to be a prophet. These five "executive branch" positions of the Body of Christ are chosen beforehand by God. What most people really want is to prophesy, which is a gift of the Holy Spirit to build up, edify, and instruct the body of Christ. Just because you have the gift of prophesy does not make you a person who stands in the office of a prophet. The Apostle Paul said, "Pursue love, and desire spiritual gifts, but especially that you may prophesy. For he who speaks in a tongue does not speak to men but to God, for no one understands him; however, in the spirit he speaks mysteries. But he who prophesies speaks edification and exhortation and comfort to men (1 Corinthians 14:1-4)."

Here is a very important protocol to be familiar with concerning the office of a prophet. The training and maturation process for this office is very intense. True prophets know the price to walk with God in this calling and would not recommend it to most people. Those who know this state of affairs sometimes attempt to get out from under it. Elijah found that out and was hiding in a cave. Jeremiah gave the Lord all kind of excuses. Moses claimed He could not talk anymore. You will be God's plumbline, measuring rod, and battle axe for a generation to whom you were called. Most people would rather not have this type of activity and would rather deal with some of the supernatural gifts that require less of a battle in the Spirit of the low impact gifts. You are God's secret agent if you are a prophet.

Prophetic succession is a very powerful way to transfer an anointing to the next generation. Having students who are genuinely called to this office is scriptural. You can get someone's else's anointed mantel by following them closely. Let us look at Elijah's protégé, Elisha. He wanted to be doubly anointed with the power from his teacher's spirit, Elijah.

"And so it was, when they had crossed over, that Elijah

said to Elisha, 'Ask! What may I do for you, before I am taken away from you?' Elisha said, 'Please let a double portion of your spirit be upon me.' So he said, 'You have asked a hard thing. Nevertheless, if you see me when I am taken from you, it shall be so for you; but if not, it shall not be so (2 Kings 2:9-11).' "

The reason that this was a hard request from Elijah was the fact that Elisha was asking for a double portion of Elijah's spirit that was in him. It does not say he wanted a double portion of what was on him. These are two different things. Never the less, Elisha stayed diligent, Elisha met the requirement of Elijah. Elisha had plenty of chances to stray, but he succeeded in seeing Elijah taken to Heaven.

And it came to pass, when the Lord was about to take up Elijah into heaven by a whirlwind, that Elijah went with Elisha from Gilgal. Then Elijah said to Elisha, "Stay here, please, for the Lord has sent me on to Bethel. "But Elisha said, "As the Lord lives, and as your soul lives, I will not leave you!" So they went down to Bethel. Now the sons of the prophets who were at Bethel came out to Elisha, and said to him, "Do you know that the Lord will take away your master from over you today?" And he said, "Yes, I know; keep silent!" Then Elijah said to him, "Elisha, stay here, please, for the Lord has sent me on to Jericho. "But he said, **"As the Lord lives, and as your soul lives, I will not leave you!"** So they came to Jericho. Now the sons of the prophets who were at Jericho came to Elisha and said to him, "Do you know that the Lord will take away your master from over you today?" So he answered, "Yes, I know; keep silent!" Then Elijah said to him, "Stay here, please, for the Lord has sent me on to the Jordan." But he said, "As the Lord lives, and as your soul lives, I will not leave you!" So the two of them went on. And fifty men of the sons of the prophets went and stood facing them at a distance, while the two of them stood by the Jordan. Now Elijah took his mantle, rolled it up, and struck the water; and it was divided this way and that, so that the two of them crossed over on dry ground. And so it was, when they had crossed over, that Elijah said to Elisha, "Ask! What may I do for you, before I am taken away from you?" Elisha said, "**Please let a double portion of your spirit be upon me** (2 Kings 2:1-9 emphasis added)!"

Your "double portion" is coming!
Be faithful to Him. It is all going to be worth it so get ready to receive it in Jesus' name.

God will place you with the proper people for the purpose of your discipleship and anointing transfer. We all need each other. God is getting us ready for His Glory to come on the earth in these days just ahead. All ministry gifts are set by the by the government of God. Even the Gifts of the Holy Spirit are given as the Spirit wills. "There are diversities of gifts, but the same Spirit. There are **differences of ministries**, but the same Lord. But one and the same Spirit works all these things, **distributing to each one individually as He wills** (1Corinthians 12:4-5,11)."

CONFRONTATION OF EVIL

When God rigs things strategically for your future, the enemy will be frustrated. He will not be comfortable around you because you carry the favor of the Lord. Remember this when the enemy comes in to confront you. It is all rigged in your favor. This is your word.

Don't move in the flesh.

41

**Wait on the Lord and let the Holy Spirit begin
to stir up your understanding. You are about to have a
miracle so stand firm and wait for the movement
of the Spirit. Let God confirm His will for you. It
was written for you a long time ago.
The divine strategies
of the Lord
are about to be revealed!
In Jesus Name.**

"Then it happened, when Ahab saw Elijah, that Ahab said to him, "Is that you, O troubler of Israel?" And he answered, "I have not troubled Israel, but you and your father's house have, in that you have forsaken the commandments of the Lord and have followed the Baals. Now therefore, send and gather all Israel to me on Mount Carmel, the four hundred and fifty prophets of Baal, and the four hundred prophets of Asherah, who eat at Jezebel's table." So Ahab sent for all the children of Israel, and gathered the prophets together on Mount Carmel. And Elijah came to all the people, and said, "How long will you falter between two opinions? If the Lord is God, follow Him; but if Baal, follow him." But the people answered him not a word. Then Elijah said to the people, "I alone am left a prophet of the Lord; but Baal's prophets are four hundred and fifty men. Therefore let them give us two bulls; and let them choose one bull for themselves, cut it in pieces, and lay it on the wood, but put no fire under it; and I will prepare the other bull, and lay it on the wood, but put no fire under it. Then you call on the name of your gods, and I will call on the name of the Lord; and the God who answers by fire, He is God (1 Kings 18:17-24)."

This is the kind of activity that will be initiated by the Holy Spirit as you seek the Lord concerning your purpose in Him. Confrontation is going to happen! Righteousness must be revealed and fulfilled. God's strategy will confront the enemy in your life. Let God stir you right now. After the stirring, build an altar. God will answer you with Fire! Elijah said to the people, "Come near to me. So all the people came near to him. And he repaired the altar of the Lord that was broken down. And Elijah took twelve stones, according to the number of the tribes of the sons of Jacob, to whom the word of the Lord had come, saying, 'Israel shall be your name (1 Kings 18:30-31)' ".

The end result of the confrontation is this: The Lord God Almighty becomes the center of worship. Let the showdown begin because the confrontation is rigged. Heaven has chosen you to be favored!

**"Then the fire of the Lord fell
and consumed the burnt sacrifice, and the wood
and the stones and the dust, and it licked up the water
that was in the trench. Now when all the people saw it,
they fell on their faces; and they said,
"The Lord, He is God! The Lord, He is God!" And Elijah
said to them, "Seize the prophets of Baal!
Do not let one of them escape!" So they seized them;
and Elijah brought them down
to the Brook Kishon and executed them there
(1 Kings 18:38-40)."**

Chapter 7

God's Secret Strategy Concerning Samson

"So the woman bore a son
and called his name Samson; and the child
grew, and the Lord blessed him. And the Spirit
of the Lord began to move upon him at
Mahaneh Dan between Zorah and
Eshtaol (Judges 13:24,25)".

The Lord will always have someone who is trained as a secret, hidden, willing, ready, agent for a mission. There are times where God desires to bring a challenge or battle to the enemy of a particular generation, even if that generation has fallen away from their God. We are in a similar situation right now. God is about to move again. It has been **forty years** since the Charismatic Move waned, and the results of that movement have all but disappeared. The year of 2017, marks the time of a new manifestation of God's goodness and glory. The glory is coming to adorn the Bride of Christ as we yield in this time of revelation, visitation, and habitation.

Again the children of Israel did evil in the sight of the Lord, and the Lord delivered them into the hand of the Philistines for forty years. Now there was a certain man from Zorah, of the family of the Danites, whose name was Manoah; and his wife was barren and had no children. And the Angel of the Lord appeared to the woman and said to her, "Indeed now, you are barren and have borne no children, but you shall conceive and bear a son. Now therefore, please be careful not to drink wine or similar drink, and not to eat anything unclean. For behold, you shall conceive and bear a son. And no razor shall come upon his head, for the child shall be a Nazirite to God from the womb; and he shall begin to deliver Israel out of the hand of the Philistines." So the woman came and told her husband, saying, "A Man of God came to me, and His countenance was like the countenance of the Angel of God, very awesome; but I did not ask Him where He was from, and He did not tell me His name. And He said to me, 'Behold, you shall conceive and bear a son. Now drink no wine or similar drink, nor eat anything unclean, for the child shall be a Nazirite to God from the womb to the day of his death.' Then Manoah prayed to the Lord, and said, 'O my Lord, please let the Man of God whom You sent come to us again and teach us what we shall do for the child who will be born (Judges 13:1-8).'

Samson was ordained by God before he was born. He was God's secret agent for God's people. Even though they had been disobedient and done evil in the sight of the Lord, God had mercy on them and sent Samson "to ...deliver

Israel out of the hand of the Philistines (Judges 13:5)." They had been in bondage to the Philistines for **forty years**.

ANGEL VISITATION

I am reminded of all the angel visitations that I have had over the years. I realize now, after looking back, that the angels came because of the urgency of secret plans of God that were about to be implemented. The angels came, not only for me personally, but for all the people in the world that God had planned to touch because of my calling and purpose that was in Christ from the foundation of the world (see Ephesians 1:3). I am interested to find out how this book will help everyone with their purpose in Him. I was sent back from death to help people in this life by activating them, through the Holy Spirit, through a heavenly impartation of revelation that flows from the Father God's heart.

Samson's parents received one of these angel visitations. They were instructed that they were no longer barren, but would have a deliverer come from them. Samson's mother was instructed that she should adhere to instructions of the angel, even down to her diet. She could affect Samson's calling even in the womb! God was about to unleash one of His agents to deliver Israel. The angel came again later and reiterated the call on their new son and his commitment to the vows that were required.

> So Manoah arose and followed his wife. When he came to the Man, he said to Him, "Are You the Man who spoke to this woman?" And He said, "I am." Manoah said, "Now let Your words come to pass! What will be the boy's rule of life, and his work?" So the Angel of the Lord said to Manoah, "Of all that I said to the woman let her be careful. She may not eat anything that comes from the vine, nor may she drink wine or similar drink, nor eat anything unclean. All that I

commanded her let her observe. ...So the woman bore a son and called his name Samson; and the child grew, and the Lord blessed him. And the Spirit of the Lord began to move upon him at Mahaneh Dan between Zorah and Eshtaol (Judges 13:11-13, 24-25).

THE SPIRIT UPON

The Spirit began to move upon Samson at Mahaneh Dan. This place was named, in English literally means, Military Camp of the Ruling Judges (see Strong's concordance, 4264, 1835, and 1777).

The Bible documents, time after time, how the Spirit of the Lord would come upon Samson and attack the Philistines. He would display supernatural strength when God told Him to do a military action and judgment against the enemies of God.

When the Holy Spirit starts to move upon someone, they will become like another person. Of course this is conditional upon the person giving themselves over to the plans and purposes of the Father. The Father, Jesus Christ, and the Holy Spirit decided long ago, to implement the wonderful things that They would perform in and through you. The ability of God to use you in this way depends upon your choice to serve Him fully, without reservation. I know this to be true, whether you accept the assignment of God or not. God does not do anything based upon our opinion or feelings about any matter. He has established your record beforehand. Just because you do not accomplish the mission, it does not diminish Him one single bit. Only those around you, in the body of Christ, suffer for your unyielding heart that refuses to allow you to move into your God given destiny.

In Him we have redemption through His blood, the forgiveness of sins, according to the riches of His grace which He made to abound toward us in all wisdom and prudence, **having made known to us the mystery of His will, according to His good pleasure which He purposed in Himself,** that in the dispensation of the fullness of the times He might gather together in one all things in Christ, both which are in heaven and which are on earth — **in Him. In Him also we have obtained an inheritance, being predestined according to the purpose of Him who works all things according to the counsel of His will,** that we who first trusted in Christ should be to the praise of His glory (Ephesians 1:7-12).

GOD'S PLEASURE

Through Samson, God executed plans of deliverance that were not known to His people. Think about this, God Almighty had a secret, hidden agenda that was not revealed until the forty years of captivity had come to an end. The mystery of His will for your life has been hidden in Christ since the foundation of the world (see Ephesians 1:4).

You are chosen for a wonderful purpose and destiny. That purpose and destiny has been hidden in Christ. The power of God is moving upon you to initiate the fulfillment of your days. Those are days of God's perfect will that are written on the pages of your book that is written about you in Heaven. "You saw me before I was born. Every day of my life was recorded in your book. Every moment was laid out before a single day had passed. How precious are your thoughts about me, O God. They cannot be numbered (Psalms 139:16-17 NLT)!"

PREDESTINED

"In Him also we have obtained an inheritance, being predestined according to the purpose of Him who works all things according to the counsel of His will, that we who first trusted in Christ should be to the praise of His glory (Ephesians 1:11-12)." It is clear by this passage of scripture that you are predestined to His purpose. He is going to work out the details of your destiny. He will counsel you by the mighty Holy Spirit, who already knows the will of God (see 1 Corinthians 2:11).

The Lord shall counsel you and keep you in His way. Trust in Him as He moves upon you for His purpose and pleasure. He loves you and wants to implement the perfect plan that was drawn up long ago for you personally.

God knew that Israel needed a deliverer and chose Samson. God used Samson to establish a battle with their oppressors. The enemy could not do anything about what the Spirit was doing, as long as Samson stayed set apart in his calling. There was one exception. The enemy could attempt to draw Samson away from his sanctified life in the purpose of God. Samson was made vulnerable when he allowed himself to be seduced by the enemy. When he joined himself with pagan companionship, he was drawn away from the fear of the Lord. He revealed the secret of his power, which was his vow to the Lord to be separated.

ACTS OF POWER

The Lord is wanting His people to yield to the power of the Resurrection in their life through what Jesus accomplished on His mission. That power will give the enemy of your soul a defeat that he will not soon forget. "... what is the

exceeding greatness of His power toward us who believe, according to the working of His mighty power which He worked in Christ when He raised Him from the dead and seated Him at His right hand in the heavenly places, far above all principality and power and might and dominion, and every name that is named, not only in this age but also in that which is to come (Ephesians 1:19-21 emphasis added). I know there is power available to those who believe. The Apostle Peter was one who was always in trouble, due to his slowness to believe and the mistakes he made with his words. Yet later, after the resurrection, his shadow would heal people of diseases as he passed by (see Acts 5:15).

My point is that He can use you, just as he has used others. What happened that men and women were suddenly used of God? THE SPIRIT MOVED ON THEM! Begin to rededicate your life to the will and heart of God. The strategies of Heaven are being revealed to you as you ask for understanding. All that you have gone through was because the enemy knew that you were destined to encounter the Holy Spirit moving on you! This generation needs you to fulfill your mission. That is why I was sent back to the earth by Jesus during my Heavenly Visitation in 1992.

Samson was clearly God's secret weapon in his time on earth. I know that you are here at this time for a similar reason. Allow the Spirit of God to have free reign in your life as the Word of God becomes alive to you. Let Him stir you in this season.

Chapter 8

God's Secret Strategy Concerning Samuel

**So Samuel grew, and the Lord
was with him and let none of his words fall to the
ground. And all Israel from Dan to Beersheba knew that
Samuel had been established as a prophet
of the Lord. Then the Lord appeared again in Shiloh.
For the Lord revealed Himself to Samuel in
Shiloh by the word of the Lord.
And the word of Samuel came to all Israel
(1 Sam 3:19-4:1 emphasis added).**

THE DEDICATION OF SAMUEL

$\mathcal{O}$ne of the most touching things that we can do, toward God, is a dedication. When we honor the Lord by acknowledging Him in all our ways, it touches His heart. With Samuel, God answered his mother's prayer one day in the Temple. Because she uttered a heartfelt, fervent prayer, she found herself pregnant with one of God's most accurate prophets to ever walk the earth. After Samuel was weaned, she immediately took the child to the Tabernacle and dedicated Him there in honor of what God did for her. She planned on leaving him there for the rest of his days. This was her doing, and it was a sacrifice beyond our understanding.

> But Hannah answered and said, "No, my lord, I am a woman of sorrowful spirit. I have drunk neither wine nor intoxicating drink, but have poured out my soul before the Lord. Do not consider your maidservant a wicked woman, for out of the abundance of my complaint and grief I have spoken until now." Then Eli answered and said, "Go in peace, and the God of Israel grant your petition which you have asked of Him." And she said, "Let your maidservant find favor in your sight." So the woman went her way and ate, and her face was no longer sad. Then they rose early in the morning and worshiped before the Lord, and returned and came to their house at Ramah. And Elkanah knew Hannah his wife, and the Lord remembered her. So it came to pass in the process of time that Hannah conceived and bore a son, and called his name Samuel, saying, "Because I have asked for him from the Lord." Now the man Elkanah and all his house went up to offer to the Lord the yearly sacrifice and his vow. But Hannah did not go up, for she said to her husband, "Not until the child is weaned; then I will take him, that he may appear before the Lord and remain there forever (1 Samuel 1:15-22)."

How many of us have a heritage of a spiritual family with spiritual parents that will do these sacred activities? I believe that you are still being prepared for your Divine strategy. The people, including Samson's parents did not even realize what Samson would do for God's Kingdom when she was praying in the Temple. God already had an answer as Hannah followed through with her vow to give Him to the Lord when it was time.

Just wanted to share the heart of the Lord on this manner. Jesus shared with me the importance of Samuel's story. Each account in the Bible is there for a very important reason. That reason is an actual seed that is planted in every generation that reads it and believes. With the truth that is planted, a harvest will appear that will change history. This story is one of those important keys in seed form.

Jesus explained to me the importance of someone who is called to be set apart in the house of the Lord. He told me that the effects the atmosphere in the house of the Lord caused him to grow up in the fear in the admonition of the Lord. He was protected from the world and its influences. The Lord said that this is key to walking in the supernatural these days as well. We may not have been shielded as much as Samuel was but the truth is still there that we need to stay separate from the world.

The Apostle Paul said to the Corinthians, "Therefore 'Come out from among them and be separate, says the Lord. Do not touch what is unclean, and I will receive you. I will be a Father to you, and you shall be My sons and daughters, says the Lord Almighty (2 Corinthians 6:17-18)."

The Jesus that I met in my Heavenly Visitation in 1992, wanted people to separate themselves from the world and become spiritual giants!

Here is the main reason Jesus shared this understanding with me. When you do not allow the spirit of the world (see 1 Corinthians 2:12) to influence your spiritual life, you will hear God clearly. Jesus assured me that staying separate from the world and its way of doing things will allow your human spirit (your inner man) to hear the Holy Spirit's voice clearly. This is not impossible. All Christians want to hear God's voice but they do not want to submit to God and resist the devil. Jesus is correct and the Apostle James affirms what Jesus said to me by writing, "Therefore submit to God. Resist the devil and he will flee from you. Draw near to God and He will draw near to you. Cleanse your hands, you sinners; and purify your hearts, you double-minded. Lament and mourn and weep! Let your laughter be turned to mourning and your joy to gloom. Humble yourselves in the sight of the Lord, and He will lift you up (James 4:7-10)."

The Jesus that I met in my **Heavenly Visitation** in 1992, wanted people to separate themselves from the world and become spiritual giants! He did not call us to Himself so that we would need to "inquire" of the Lord through a prophet. God will use the ministry gifts to confirm something that you have been already partially or fully realized, but you are not led by prophets as sons of God. The Bible says that, "For as many as are led by the Spirit of God, these are sons of God (Romans 8:14-15)!"

Please, always remember that you are His children, His sheep in His care. We can hear His voice. "For He is our God, and we are the people of His pasture, and the sheep of His hand. Today, if you will hear His voice: "Do not harden your hearts, as in the rebellion, as in the day of trial in the wilderness, (Psalm 95:7-8)."

I might add this fact: Jesus, Himself said, "My sheep hear My voice, and I know them, and they follow Me. And I give them eternal life, and they shall never perish; neither shall anyone snatch them out of My hand. My Father, who has given them to Me, is greater than all; and no one is able to snatch them out of My Father's hand. I and My Father are one (John 10:27-30)."

The Father loves us, and He wants to speak to us. He has spoken to us through His Son, Jesus. Jesus sent the Holy Spirit to us, and He speaks to us about Jesus (John 15:26). So there is a dialogue that has been established between us and the Trinity. If we are not hearing, it is because we need to work on the receiving end.

God did not call you to seek out what others are saying regarding the future so that you can say you observed history being made. He called you, personally, to hear from Him, yourself and act out your destiny by the Spirit. He has called you to be a history-maker. You are not an observer. You are an implementer of history ! It's all rigged in your favor!

MINISTERING TO THE LORD

One of the key practices of Samuel's life that Jesus pointed out to me was the fact that he ministered to the Lord. I was surprised when I met Jesus face-to-face. A lot of things about His personality caused me to change my way of thinking. I felt as though He had been misrepresented on the earth. The Bible was correct, but many interpretations concerning Him were not. The Father and the His Son, Jesus, love to be worshipped. They want to hear you say heartfelt words of adoration, and They want to know about your reliance on them. Samuel learned to do this in the Tabernacle. "Now the boy Samuel ministered to the Lord before Eli. And the word of the Lord was rare in those days; there was no widespread revelation. And it came to pass at that time, while Eli was lying down in his place, and when his eyes had begun to grow so dim that he could not see, and before the lamp of God went out in the tabernacle of the

Lord where the ark of God was, and while Samuel was lying down, that the Lord called Samuel. And he answered, "Here I am!" So he ran to Eli and said, "Here I am, for you called me (1 Samuel 3:1-5)." I want to emphasize that the "Word of the Lord was rare in those days." The fact that Samuel heard the Lord made it all the more significant. God was speaking because of Samuel's dedication, and because of his ministry to the Lord. We can all do this. Jesus has assured me of this.

HEAR, THEN SPEAK WITH ACCURACY

The main purpose for Samuel's life was for God's voice to be heard in a generation that had been experiencing silence from Heaven. In God's secret strategies, Samuel was raised up to be a prophet and a priest of the Most High. The Lord also appeared to Him at Shiloh (From Strong's concordance #7951; tranquil; Shiloh, an epithet of the Messiah). God began to speak to Samuel. In turn, Samuel began to speak to the people on behalf of God. "So Samuel grew, and the Lord was with him and let none of his words fall to the ground. And all Israel from Dan to Beersheba knew that Samuel had been established as a prophet of the Lord. Then the Lord appeared again in Shiloh. For the Lord revealed Himself to Samuel in Shiloh by the Word of the Lord. And the word of Samuel came to all Israel (1 Sam 3:19-4:1 emphasis added)."

The Lord's voice was a secret strategy from Heaven. He had preordained that Samuel would bring this to his generation. Because of the honor of His parents toward the Lord, and later the honor of Samuel himself, expressed, God was able to have a man in place that ruled from heaven over God's people with extreme accuracy. You have your place in this generation. May God reveal His strategy for your life as you continue to read this book.

Chapter 9

God's Secret Strategy Concerning David

David was an innocent boy who probably did not know all that God had in store for Him. As he sat on the hills of the countryside, keeping his father's sheep, he had plenty of solitude. This gave God opportunity to interact with him at a very young age. David did not know it at the time, but he was in training to be the King of Israel. God knew the series of events that would transpire concerning Israel's desire to have a King as the other nations around them. That grieved God because He wanted to be their King. He reluctantly gave them their request by having Samuel anoint Saul to be their ruler. As you know, this did not work out because Saul was disobedient. David was chosen instead. The Messiah was prophesied to come through David's lineage.

HIDDEN FOR GOD

David's life was God's secret agenda for His plan. David was called to rule and reign, not only to his generation, but also throughout all generations. David said, "...that the Lord may fulfill His word which He spoke concerning me, saying, 'If your sons take heed to their way, to walk before Me in truth with all their heart and with all their soul,' He said, 'you shall not lack a man on the throne of Israel (1 Kings 2:4).' "

God's will for you is that you will leave a legacy to the next generation. God is moving on your behalf, not just for you or the people around you, but for the next generation as well. God is wanting to make an impact through every child that He may call.

David was out tending sheep because God wanted him to attend sheep. This atmosphere was God's choice for training. God's secret strategy, for future missions, was to destroy the offspring of the Nephilim that had mysteriously appeared again after the flood.

> Now it came to pass, when men began to multiply on the face of the earth, and daughters were born to them, that the sons of God saw the daughters of men, that they were beautiful; and they took wives for themselves of all whom they chose. And the Lord said, "My Spirit shall not strive with man forever, for he is indeed flesh; yet his days shall be one hundred and twenty years." There were giants on the earth in those days, **and also afterward**, when the sons of

God came in to the daughters of men and they bore children to them. Those were the mighty men who were of old, men of renown (Genesis 6:1-4 emphasis added).

As you can see by the previous passage, God already knew that these beings would reappear. God is never caught off guard. He ordained that David would rise up and accomplish the task of the destruction of the Nephilim. David would carry out God's mission for their ultimate demise. David was chosen before the situation even came into being. He was being trained by watching sheep for his father. The whole time, God was the One who prepared for him to be a warrior, psalmist, prophet, priest and king.

THE WARRIOR

As David grew older, he was anointed by Samuel to be king of Israel. The Spirit of the Lord was on him from that day forth. There was a delay before David was able to become the king of Israel because Saul was still in power, even though God had rejected him. When the anointing oil was applied, God activated the strategies of Heaven upon David. "So as David stood there among his brothers, Samuel took the flask of olive oil he had brought and anointed David with the oil. And the Spirit of the Lord came powerfully upon David from that day on. Then Samuel returned to Ramah (1 Samuel 16:13 NLT emphasis added)."

One day, David fulfilled part of God's destiny for him and the people of Israel. The hidden strategy that God used had been developing as David was keeping the sheep. His father asked him to take supplies to the frontlines of a battle that was going on with the Philistines. So David obeyed his father and took supplies to his brothers.

So David rose early in the morning, left the sheep with a keeper, and took the things and went as Jesse had commanded him. And he came to the camp as the army was going out to the fight and shouting for the battle. For Israel and the Philistines had drawn up in battle array, army against army. And David left his supplies in the hand of the supply keeper, ran to the army, and came and greeted his brothers. Then as he talked with them, there was the champion, the Philistine of Gath, Goliath by name, coming up from the armies of the Philistines; and he spoke according to the same words. So David heard them. And all the men of Israel, when they saw the man, fled from him and were dreadfully afraid. So the men of Israel said, "Have you seen this man who has come up? Surely he has come up to defy Israel; and it shall be that the man who kills him the king will enrich with great riches, will give him his daughter, and give his father's house exemption from taxes in Israel." Then David spoke to the men who stood by him, saying, "What shall be done for the man who kills this Philistine and takes away the reproach from Israel? For who is this uncircumcised Philistine, that he should defy the armies of the living God?" ...And Saul said to David, "You are not able to go against this Philistine to fight with him; for you are a youth, and he a man of war from his youth." But David said to Saul, "Your servant used to keep his father's sheep, and when a lion or a bear came and took a lamb out of the flock, I went out after it and struck it, and delivered the lamb from its mouth; and when it arose against me, I caught it by its beard, and struck and killed it. Your servant has killed both lion and bear; and this uncircumcised Philistine will be like one of them, seeing he has defied the armies of the living God." Moreover David said, "The Lord, who delivered me from the paw of the lion and from the paw of the bear, He will deliver me from the hand of this Philistine (1 Sam 17:20-26,33-37)!

The end result was that David became a war hero that day in the eyes of man. But in the eyes of God, David was a war hero even before He was born. In Genesis, chapter six, God already knew He needed a giant-killer named David.

See yourself in the same type of situation that David experienced. He was just doing his job with the sheep, and then God unveiled His destiny. He used David's job to train him, and He used your experience to train you also. One day, when the timing is right, you will rise to the occasion. It will all come clear. There is a Samuel waiting to ordain you with a flask of anointing oil, there is a war brewing that you will enter. You will slay the giant!

THE PSALMIST

There is no doubt that David, along with his sling shot, had a harp in his hand and played continually during his watch over the sheep. The Spirit of the Lord was on him and the songs just flowed. Many psalms were written by David and recorded in the Bible. They are a secret weapon of God for all the future generations. One of the amazing, secret weapons involving the harp, was revealed one day when King Saul called on David. "And Saul's servants said to him, 'Surely, a distressing spirit from God is troubling you. Let our master now command your servants, who are before you, to seek out a man who is a skillful player on the harp. And it shall be that he will play it with his hand when the distressing spirit from God is upon you, and you shall be well.' So Saul said to his servants, 'Provide me now a man who can play well, and bring him to me.' Then one of the servants answered and said, 'Look, I have seen a son of Jesse the Bethlehemite, who is skillful in playing, a mighty man of valor, a man of war, prudent in speech, and a handsome person; and the Lord is with him.' ...And so it was, whenever the spirit from God was upon Saul, that David would take a harp and play it with his hand. Then Saul would become refreshed and well, and the distressing spirit would depart from him (1 Sam 16:15-18, 23)."

One of David's gifts from God sent evil spirits fleeing! This is a profound mystery, but God was beginning to reveal His plan. Remember this point: anointed music drives out evil spirits whether you understand it, or not. Do not let the enemy discourage you, if you are to play a musical instrument. You could be a secret weapon against the enemy! We need to fulfill our directives from the Lord so that the Body of Christ is built up and we become one.

THE KING

David eventually sat on his throne and ruled Israel. He loved the Kingdom of God that was established in Israel. God gave favor while he was king and promised that his descendants would rule on the throne forever. God may have you in His government as a leader. You may be called as one of the five-fold offices of the church (Apostles, Prophets, Pastors, Evangelist, and Teachers). Either way, The Apostle Paul said that we "...will reign in life through the One, Jesus Christ (see Romans 5:17)." The bottom line is that righteousness and justice reigned while David was on the throne. "I will sing of the mercies of the Lord forever; with my mouth will I make known Your faithfulness to all generations. For I have said, "Mercy shall be built up forever; Your faithfulness You shall establish in the very heavens. I have made a covenant with My chosen, I have sworn to My servant David: 'Your seed I will establish forever, and build up your throne to all generations. Selah. And the heavens will praise Your wonders, O Lord; Your faithfulness also in the assembly of the saints. For who in the heavens can be compared to the Lord? Who among the sons of the mighty can be likened to the Lord? God is greatly to be feared in the assembly of the saints, and to be held in reverence by all those around Him. O Lord God of hosts, Who is mighty like You, O Lord? Your faithfulness also surrounds You. I have found My servant David; with My holy oil I have anointed him, With whom My hand shall be established; Also My arm shall strengthen him. The enemy shall not outwit him, nor the son of wickedness afflict him. I will beat down his foes before his face, and plague those who hate him. 'But My faithfulness and My mercy shall be with him, and in My name his horn shall be exalted (Psalm 89: 1-8, 20-24)."

THE PROPHET

Many of David's Psalms were written as prophecies of the Messiah Jesus. David was going through tough times in his life and would write about it in song form. Later, we realize that he was revealing the exact encounters, quotes, and even thoughts, of Jesus. Here is an example of David, the prophet, prophesying, the crucifixion in great detail many years before Jesus came to earth in bodily form. Notice that Jesus even quotes David word-for-word.

My God, my God, why have you abandoned me? Why are you so far away when I groan for help? Every day I call to you, my God, but you do not answer. Every night you hear my voice, but I find no relief. Yet you are holy, enthroned on the praises of Israel. Our ancestors trusted in you, and you rescued them. They cried out to you and were saved. They trusted in you and were never disgraced. But I am a worm and not a man. I am scorned and despised by all! Everyone who sees me mocks me. They sneer and shake their heads, saying, "Is this the one who relies on the Lord? Then let the Lord save him! If the Lord loves him so much, let the Lord rescue him!" Yet you brought me safely from my mother's womb and led me to trust you at my mother's breast. I was thrust into your arms at my birth. You have been my God from the moment I was born. Do not stay so far from me, for trouble is near, and no one else can help me. My enemies surround me like a herd of bulls; fierce bulls of Bashan have hemmed me in! Like lions they open their jaws against me, roaring and tearing into their prey. My life is poured out like water, and all my bones are out of joint. My heart is like wax, melting within me. My strength has dried up like sunbaked clay. My tongue sticks to the roof of my mouth. You have laid me in the dust and left me for dead. My enemies surround me like a pack of dogs; an evil gang closes in on me. They have pierced my hands and feet. I can count all my bones. My enemies stare at me and gloat. They divide my garments among themselves and throw dice for my clothing. O Lord, do not stay far away! You are my strength; come quickly to my aid! Save me from the sword; spare my precious life from these dogs. Snatch me from the lion's jaws and from the horns of these wild oxen. I will proclaim your name to my brothers and sisters. I will praise you among your assembled people. Praise the Lord, all you who fear him! Honor him, all you descendants of Jacob! Show him reverence, all you descendants of Israel! For he has not ignored or belittled the suffering of the needy. He has not turned his back on them, but has listened to their cries for help. I will praise you in the great assembly. I will fulfill my vows in the presence of those who worship you. The poor will eat and be satisfied. All who seek the Lord will praise him. Their hearts will rejoice with everlasting joy. The whole earth will acknowledge the Lord and return to him. All the families of the nations will bow down before him. For royal power belongs to the Lord. He rules all the nations. Let the rich of the earth feast and worship. Bow before him, all who are mortal, all whose lives will end as dust. Our children will also serve him. Future generations will hear about the wonders of the Lord. His righteous acts will be told to those not yet born. They will hear about everything he has done (Psalms 22:1-31 NLT).

THE PRIEST

David was also known to enter the tabernacle with the ephod and inquire of the Lord as a priest. This was a secret weapon that led to many miracles because of the guidance he received while wearing the priest's ephod. He presented offers and performed other duties of a priest. "Then David said to Abiathar the priest, Ahimelech's son, 'Please bring the ephod here to me.' And Abiathar brought the ephod to David. So David inquired of the Lord, saying, 'Shall I pursue this troop? Shall I overtake them?' And He answered him, 'Pursue, for you shall surely overtake them and without fail recover all (1 Sam 30:7-8).' "

David was an example to us. We have been made kings and priests through Jesus Christ. The Apostle John said, "To Him who loved us and washed us from our sins in His own blood, and has made us kings and priests to His God and Father, to Him be glory and dominion forever and ever. Amen (Revelation 1:5-6)."

David certainly was a weapon in the hand of the Lord on many fronts. Let us take up the same faith as David did by believing that God is working out everything concerning you this day. God will not waste your life, but He will utilize it. The Spirit of the Lord has many things to tell you as you wait on Him.

Chapter 10

God's Secret Strategy Concerning Jesus

When Jesus came to the earth through the womb of Mary, He was the Preexisting One. We seem to have forgotten that Jesus came to earth to redeem us from a position of being equal to God. The Apostle Paul said, "Let this mind be in you, which was also in Christ Jesus: Who, being in the form of God, thought it not robbery to be equal with God: But made himself of no reputation, and took upon him the form of a servant, and was made in the likeness of men: And being found in fashion as a man, he humbled himself, and became obedient unto death, even the death of the cross (Philippians 2:5-8 KJV)."

Jesus, along with the rest of the Trinity, knew that He was going to come to the earth with the mission of defeating the enemy. The secret agenda of God was to come as a man and live a life without sin so that He would be ready to be a perfect sacrifice, to die in our place. All that believe in Him shall be saved! The Apostle John said, "He who sins is of the devil, for the devil has sinned from the beginning. **For this purpose the Son of God was manifested, that He might destroy the works of the devil** (1 John 3:8-9 emphasis added).

This salvation was the wonderful plan from the foundation of the world (see 1 Peter 1:20). The enemy did not understand what was happening. God Almighty had a secret strategy hidden in the plan of the Messiah, and that was death! The devil did not know this, and God won the victory of death, hell, and the grave. It was a divine setup according to the Apostle Paul who wrote, "However, we speak wisdom among those who are mature, yet not the wisdom of this age, nor of the rulers of this age, who are coming to nothing. But we speak the wisdom of God in a mystery, the hidden wisdom which God ordained before the ages for our glory, which none of the rulers of this age knew; for had they known, they would not have crucified the Lord of glory (1 Corinthians 2:6-8 emphasis added)."

The Word of God says that Jesus destroyed the works of the devil. All of this was possible because it was preplanned from the beginning. It is all rigged in your favor as you submit to God and resist the devil (see James 4:7).

THE POOL OF BETHESDA

There many things that we could talk about in this chapter. One story that stands out is the pool of Bethesda. Jesus taught me at length about this, and so I will share this understanding with you briefly.

One of the most important topics that the Lord has explained to me in visitations is our inability to discern spiritually what is right in front of us. We miss so many opportunities because we are not praying to have ears that hear and eyes that see in the Spirit realm. May God give us a quickening of our spiritual senses by the powerful Holy Spirit.

> After this there was a feast of the Jews; and Jesus went up to Jerusalem. Now there is at Jerusalem by the sheep market a pool, which is called in the Hebrew tongue Bethesda, having five porches. In these lay a great multitude of impotent folk, of blind, halt, withered, waiting for the moving of the water. For an angel went down at a certain season into the pool, and troubled the water: whosoever then first after the troubling of the water stepped in was made whole of whatsoever disease he had. And a certain man was there, which had an infirmity thirty and eight years. When Jesus saw him lie, and knew that he had been now a long time in that case, he saith unto him, Wilt thou be made whole? The impotent man answered him, Sir, I have no man, when the water is troubled, to put me into the pool: but while I am coming, another steppeth down before me. Jesus saith unto him, Rise, take up thy bed, and walk. And immediately the man was made whole, and took up his bed, and walked: and on the same day was the Sabbath (John 5:1-9 KJV).

The man at the pool did not discern his day of visitation until it was revealed to him. Jesus had many times warned His disciples about being spiritually dull. At times they did not receive spiritual truth. Jesus even went as far as speaking over Jerusalem itself. He said,"...If you had known, even you, especially in this your day, the things that make for your peace! But now they are hidden from your eyes. For days will come upon you when your enemies will build an embankment around you, surround you and close you in on every side, and level you, and your children within you, to the ground; and they will not leave in you one stone upon another, **because you did not know the time of your**

visitation (Luke 19:42-44 emphasis added)."

When you discern who Jesus is, you can partake of Him in that area of your life. Jesus is the "Bread" that came down from Heaven (see John 6:58). Jesus taught me to have my inner man (my born-again spirit) actively listening at all times. He instructed me to refrain from being carnal and immature as the Apostle Paul talked about in I Corinthians 3:1).

Jesus comes to you daily in many ways. He wants you to be more discerning spiritually. Jesus showed me that most people are as the man at the pool. They would want Jesus to help them in the pool when the water was stirred by an angel. All the time, Jesus was the Messiah, and He could heal them immediately.

To become more spiritually sharp, means that you are going to need quality time, feeding on the supernatural Word of God. This is done by meditating on what God has said in the Bible. Then, you must allow the atmosphere of Heaven to invade your world by praying in the Spirit and allowing the Peace of God to rule.

Jesus is the destroyer of our enemy, the devil. He truly loves us. Let Him teach you how to be overcomers. We will discern our day of visitation as we see the tables turned on our enemy. God had our victory planned out long ago. Receive from Jesus now.

**But you, beloved, building yourselves
up on your most holy faith, praying in the Holy Spirit,
keep yourselves in the love of God, looking
for the mercy of our Lord Jesus Christ
unto eternal life (Jude 1: 20-21).**

Chapter 11

God's Secret Strategy Concerning The Holy Spirit

When the Day of Pentecost had fully come,
they were all with one accord in one place. And
suddenly there came a sound from heaven, as of a rushing
mighty wind, and it filled the whole house where they were
sitting. Then there appeared to them divided tongues,
as of fire, and one sat upon each of them. And they
were all filled with the Holy Spirit and began to
speak with other tongues, as the Spirit gave
them utterance (Acts 2:1-4).

God's hidden strategy for us concerning the Holy Spirit has been an amazing revelation to me from the Word of God. We have so much for which to be thankful when it comes to the person of the Holy Spirit. He has such a strong character of Jesus as He breathes on you. He gives us abilities that are supernatural in order to build up the body of Christ. He causes us to tesify about Jesus to the lost and see them come into The Faith.

Unity

We know the Lord by the revelation of His Word. We can understand that the Trinity knows each other intimately. There is an absolute agreement between each of them.

When the earth realm fell, there began to be changes in everything because of the curse. Eventually, because of sin and man's inclination to perform evil, man had to be restricted. Man was in agreement with each other, and man was forming larger groups of people. One particular strategy of the Lord was to confuse their languages so they could not communicate with each other. This caused division and separation of the human race. God had no choice. Because of their fallen condition, He decided to do this so that it would slow down their evil plans against Him.

The Lord looked down and saw that man was evil. One day the Trinity had this to say about the condition of mankind on the earth.

> Now the whole earth had one language and one speech. And it came to pass, as they journeyed from the east, that they found a plain in the land of Shinar, and they dwelt there. Then they said to one another, "Come, let us make bricks and bake them thoroughly." They had brick for stone, and they had asphalt for mortar. And they said, "Come, let us build ourselves a city, and a tower whose top is in the heavens; **let us make a name for ourselves**, lest we be scattered abroad over the face of the whole earth." But the Lord came down to see the city and the tower which the sons of men had built. And the Lord said, "Indeed the people are one and they all have one language, and this is what they

begin to do; **now nothing that they propose to do will be withheld from them.** Come, let Us go down and there confuse their language, that they may not understand one another's speech." So the Lord scattered them abroad from there over the face of all the earth, and they ceased building the city. Therefore its name is called Babel, because there the Lord confused the language of all the earth; and from there the Lord scattered them abroad over the face of all the earth (Genesis 11:1-9).

God confused their language, and that is the way it has been since that time in the secular world. However, in the Spiritual world involving the Kingdom of God, we encounter an event called the Outpouring of the Holy Spirit. It happened a little over two thousand years ago on the Day of Pentecost. This reversed the curse in Genesis 11, by reuniting us in the language of the Spirit.

And there were dwelling in Jerusalem Jews, devout men, from every nation under heaven. And when this sound occurred, the multitude came together, and were confused, because everyone heard them speak in his own language. Then they were all amazed and marveled, saying to one another, "Look, are not all these who speak Galileans? And how is it that we hear, each in our own language in which we were born? Parthians and Medes and Elamites, those dwelling in Mesopotamia, Judea and Cappadocia, Pontus and Asia, Phrygia and Pamphylia, Egypt and the parts of Libya adjoining Cyrene, visitors from Rome, both Jews and proselytes, Cretans and Arabs — **we hear them speaking in our own tongues the wonderful works of God** (Acts 2:5-12 emphasis added).

The Lord reversed the curse of Babel on the Day of Pentecost. Now, in the Spirit, we can speak as the Spirit gives utterance. The Holy Spirit causes us to have one mind and one heart as we walk in love toward each other. The Holy Sprit provides the nine supernatural gifts of the Holy Spirit to edify and build up the body of believers.

The Apostle Paul wrote to the Ephesians saying, "I, therefore, the prisoner of the Lord, beseech you to walk worthy of the calling with which you were called, with all lowliness and gentleness, with longsuffering, bearing with one another in love, endeavoring to keep the unity of the Spirit in the bond of peace. There is one body and one Spirit, just as you were called in one hope of your calling; one Lord, one faith, one baptism; one God and Father of all, who is above all, and through all, and in you all (Ephesians 4:1-6)."

The Lord had a secret, divine strategy hidden until the proper time. The Spirit of God is used to bring harmony from chaos. He turned the tables on the enemy for us. Now we must seek peace and pursue it. We are one in the Spirit of God as we yield to Him. You can understand why the enemy tries to stop the Holy Spirit from being poured out upon us and manifested in our midst. He is no match for the unified Body of Christ.

Chapter 12

God's Secret Strategy Concerning The Glory

The Glory contains the righteousness and holiness of God. When the Glory of God comes into a place, there will be no flesh able to stand prideful in His presence. All work will cease. Questions will be answered because He is the answer. Any type of physical ailments will be driven from the body.

All oppressive evil spirits will flee away. Your spiritual senses will be heightened to the place that you will see things you never did before. You will rest in the Glory. There is indescribable peace in His Glory. God will give you the grace to repent and see that He is good. All of your needs will be met in the Glory.

Bodies will begin to be repaired as healing flows. All things must line up with the perfect will of God. You will hear bones and joints popping into place as correction comes. People will repent because of the revelation that God is a good God.

The Glory is what accompanies the Father. He has given it to the Son, Jesus. You will see things about the Father that you never knew. You will have a revelation of His Grace. His favor will become alive in you as your angelic escorts take you into the Land of Favor. Moses saw His glory, and the people made him cover his face because he started to resemble his Creator, the One that made him in His Own Image was before him. We will see that we are one as Jesus and the Father are One. God will come by and announce His name to us. The fear of the Lord will return to us; it is the beginning of Wisdom. Then you will see the Ultimate:

God Calls You His Friend!
Welcome To The Glory of God!

ABOUT THE AUTHOR

Kevin Zadai was called to ministry at the age of ten. He attended Central Bible College in Springfield, Missouri, where he received a Bachelor of Arts in Theology. Later, he received training in Missions at Rhema Bible College. He is currently ordained through Rev. Dr. Jesse and Rev. Dr. Cathy Duplantis. At age thirty-one, during a routine day surgery, he found himself on the 'other side of the veil' with Jesus. For forty-five minutes, the Master revealed spiritual truths before returning him to his body and assigning him to a supernatural ministry. Kevin holds a Commercial Pilot license and has been employed by Southwest Airlines for twenty-nine years as a flight attendant. He and his lovely wife, Kathi, reside in New Orleans, Louisiana.

SALVATION PRAYER

LORD GOD,
I CONFESS THAT I AM A SINNER. I
CONFESS THAT I NEED YOUR SON
JESUS. PLEASE FORGIVE ME IN HIS
NAME.

LORD JESUS, I BELIEVE YOU
DIED FOR ME AND THAT YOU ARE
ALIVE AND LISTENING TO ME NOW.

I NOW TURN FROM MY SINS, AND
WELCOME YOU INTO MY HEART.
COME AND TAKE CONTROL OF MY
LIFE. MAKE ME THE KIND OF
PERSON YOU WANT ME TO BE.

NOW, FILL ME WITH YOUR HOLY
SPIRIT, WHO WILL SHOW ME HOW
TO LIVE FOR YOU. I
ACKNOWLEDGE YOU BEFORE MEN
AS MY SAVIOR AND MY LORD.

IN JESUS' NAME.
AMEN.

IF YOU PRAYED THIS PRAYER. PLEASE CONTACT US AT
info@warriornotes.com for more information and material.

Please look for the companion
study guide and prayer guide for this particular
book. This is volume two of the Heavenly
Encounters Series.

Go to warriornotes.com for other exciting ministry
materials.

Warriornotes.com

Made in the USA
Middletown, DE
26 March 2017